Oranges grow on trees, but do bananas?

Do sharks need to keep swimming in order to breathe?

WHY EVERYTHING YOU KNOW IS WRONG!

SCHOLASTIC

CONTENTS

CLASSIC MISTAKES!

Age-old errors — from bulls seeing red and deserts being sandy, to the idea that houseflies live for just one day.

JUST PLAIN WRONG!

The real truth about Apollo spacecraft landing on the moon, swallowing gum, and dropping food on the floor.

EVERYBODY THINKS SO!

Who says carrots are good for your eyes? Does shaving make your hair grow thicker? Were dinosaurs really giant lizards?

CHAPTER 4   68–91

IT'S COMPLICATED!

Dig deeper to see how gravity works in space, why the blood in your veins isn't really blue, and how chameleons change color.

CHAPTER 5   92–103

MEDIA MIX-UPS!

Debunk misleading media myths about suicidal lemmings, humans walking with dinosaurs, and Newton's apple.

CHAPTER 6   104–125

BUT IT SOUNDS TRUE!

Don't believe all you hear about sugar making you hyperactive, polar bears having white fur, or spiders being deadly.

*A housefly lives for just one day.
Seriously? Not everything you've
been told is true. In some cases,
people have been making the
same mistakes for years.*

CLASSIC MISTAKES!

 **WRONG!** There is only one north pole.

A COMPASS NEEDLE POINTS TOWARD THE NORTH MAGNETIC POLE, WHICH IS ABOUT 750 MILES (1,200 KM) AWAY FROM THE TRUE NORTH POLE.

Satellite navigation systems do not use **compasses** to show where you are going. You can set them to point to **Magnetic North** or **True North**. **It's up to you!**

WHAT HAPPENS TO COMPASSES AT THE NORTH POLE?

When explorers get close to the true North Pole, their magnetic compasses stop working. The needle wants to point straight down, but can't. Instead, it swings around pointing to any iron objects in the area.

NORTH 90°N POLE

The **true (or geographic) North Pole** is a point on Earth's surface around which the planet **spins once every 24 hours**. (So is the **South Pole** on the globe's other end.)

Earth is a **giant magnet! The solid metal core** is surrounded by **swirling liquid iron,** creating a magnetic field. But the magnetic and geographic poles don't match up.

The **North Magnetic Pole** never **stays still.** At the moment, it is very close to Ellesmere Island in Canada, and **moving west by about 25 miles (40 km) every year.**

Earth's magnetism traps plasma (superhot gas) streaming out of the sun and **pulls it toward the poles.** When it hits the atmosphere, the plasma produces lights, or an **aurora**, in the sky.

The sea looks blue because it reflects the sky.

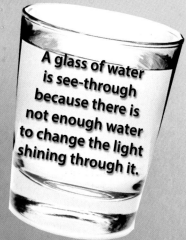

A glass of water is see-through because there is not enough water to change the light shining through it.

THREE COLORFUL FACTS

- An **iceberg** is white because of tiny air bubbles that are trapped in the water as it **freezes.** When very pure water freezes, it makes beautiful blue ice.

- No one knows where the **Red Sea** between Egypt and Arabia **got its name.** However, it might be from an **unusual plankton** that sometimes grows there, which makes the water go red.

- About 3,000 feet (900 m) below the surface, the **ocean is not blue;** it is black because it is completely dark all the time.

THE SEA DOES NOT REFLECT
THE SKY, BUT IT IS BLUE FOR
THE SAME REASON — THE
WAY IT EITHER ABSORBS
OR BOUNCES BACK THE
COLORS IN SUNLIGHT.

WHY DO BOTH THE SEA AND THE SKY LOOK BLUE?

Sunlight is white, a mixture of all the colors of the rainbow. When it shines into deep water, the red, green, and yellow light is all absorbed. However, the blue light bounces back and that is what our eyes pick up — so to us, the ocean, like the sky, looks blue.

ASTRONAUTS HAVE LOOKED FOR THE GREAT WALL, BUT THEY CAN'T SEE IT WITHOUT USING A TELESCOPE.

The Great Wall of China is **5,500 miles (8,850 km) long.**

The wall we see today took nearly **1,700 years to construct** and was built to **stop invaders from Mongolia.**

WHAT CAN YOU SEE FROM SPACE?

Astronauts can see huge dams, immense mines, and the world's biggest buildings. After dark, they can see lights from big cities.

WRONG!

The Great Wall of China is the only man-made feature visible from space.

The idea that you could see **the Great Wall from space** was started by English archaeologist William Stukeley in 1754. He said it was **so big you could see it from the moon!**

In 2003, **China launched its first astronaut. Yang Liwei confirmed that the Great Wall was not visible.**

Although it is very long, the wall is only about **30 feet (9 m) wide.**

 **WRONG!** Everyone thought
the world was flat
until Columbus
went exploring.

IN 1492, MOST
EXPERTS
AGREED THAT
THE PLANET WAS
A SPHERE, AND
HAD THOUGHT SO
FOR 2,000 YEARS.

Ancient Greek scientists knew **Earth must be a sphere** because during a **lunar eclipse, Earth's shadow covers the moon.** The **shadow is round,** and only a **sphere always casts round shadows.**

The first person to measure the size of Earth was **Eratosthenes,** in **200 BCE.**

The first person to **sail around the world** was Juan Sebastián Elcano, the captain of the surviving ship on Magellan's 1519 expedition.

The **first photo** of the **curvature of Earth** was taken by *Explorer II,* **in 1935.**

When an **airplane flies** in what looks to be a **straight line over the surface of Earth,** it is **actually moving in a curve.**

The **curvature of Earth** prevents you seeing **as far as** you would be able to see if the **world was flat.** To see farther, you have to **climb higher.**

 Black panthers and leopards are different species.

A BLACK PANTHER IS A SPECIAL KIND OF LEOPARD. IT STILL HAS DARK SPOTS, BUT THE REST OF ITS FUR IS DARK, TOO, SO YOU CANNOT SEE THEM.

The black **panther's** fur is made **dark** by a chemical called **melanin,** which is the same **stuff** that **makes human skin dark.**

The word **panther** comes from **Greek words** that mean **"killer of all animals."**

Leopards are **big cats** that **hunt** mainly at night. They live in **Africa** and **Asia**. Most **black leopards**, however, **live in Asian rain forests.**

There are **black panthers** living in **South America** as well, only this time they are **dark jaguars.**

A leopard's **spots** make good **camouflage during the day,** when it is **resting** in the **shadows under trees.** Completely **black fur** makes a cat more **visible** to predators.

 **WRONG!**

People only use 10% of their brains.

WE DON'T USE 100 PERCENT OF OUR BRAIN ALL THE TIME, BUT WE USE DIFFERENT PARTS OF IT FOR DIFFERENT THINGS — IT ALL GETS USED.

The human brain needs one-fifth of the energy used by the body to keep working. It uses energy even when you are asleep.

DID YOU KNOW?

○ There are about 86 billion nerve cells in a human brain. Every nerve cell, or **neuron,** is connected to thousands of others. That means a brain has about **several hundred trillion connections!**

○ The surface of the **human brain** is heavily folded. Laid out flat, the surface of a human brain would cover **two newspaper pages.**

○ The brain is made from gray matter and white matter. **Gray matter** processes information. **White matter** sends signals between areas of gray matter.

Albert Einstein is supposed to have said his great intelligence came from using more of his brain than other people did, so maybe that's where we get this wrong idea.

 **WRONG!** Houseflies have a life span of 24 hours.

HOUSEFLIES DO NOT LIVE LONG, BUT IT'S MORE LIKE A MONTH THAN A DAY.

DID YOU KNOW?

- Flies **throw up** on their food to soften it up before they eat it, and defecate every four to five minutes. **Yuck!** No wonder no one wants them around food!

- Flies can walk upside down thanks to **glue** that oozes from the pads on their **toes.**

- Flies **smell** with their antennae and **taste** with their feet!

- A baby fly, or **maggot**, lives in **garbage** and even yuckier stuff (poop) and is ready to become an adult in less than **36 hours.**

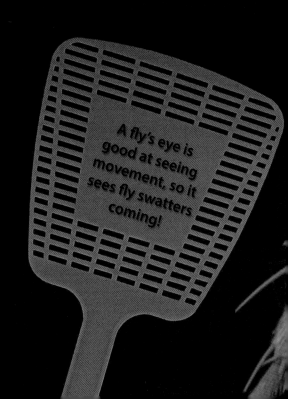

A fly's eye is good at seeing movement, so it sees fly swatters coming!

 **Bulls are enraged by the color red.**

A BULL CANNOT EVEN SEE THE COLOR RED. WHEN THE MATADOR WAVES HIS CAPE, THE BULL IS CHARGING AT THE MOVEMENT OF THE CAPE.

Bulls have been **used in sports** for **thousands of years.** Athletes from the Minoan culture from 2000 BCE Crete, did somersaults over charging bulls! Competitors **grabbed a bull's horns** and used them to flip over the animal's back.

HOW DO WE KNOW WHAT THE WORLD LOOKS LIKE TO ANIMALS?

The eye detects colors with cells known as cones. The chemicals in an animal's cones tell scientists what colors they can see. We can then recreate how the world would look using just those colors.

Having **eyes** on both sides of the head **gives a cow almost 360-degree vision** — but it can't see size and shape clearly.

Rhinos charge at any threat, but they have very **bad eyesight** and have been known to **attack termite mounds and head-butt trees**.

Cattle, like most mammals, can **only see two colors**. Their eyes can detect **blue** and they see **green** and **yellow** as shades of blue. Red things appear gray.

 **Deserts are mostly made of sand.**

The **largest desert in the world** is **not the Sahara** in North Africa, **it is Antarctica.** It **almost never rains** there and all the **water** is **frozen solid.**

The **tallest sand dunes** in the world are in **China's Badain Jaran desert.** They are over **1,640 feet (500 m) high.**

The Salar de Uyuni in Bolivia is the **world's largest salt flat desert.** It's about the size of Connecticut. **This desert** is also the **flattest place on Earth.**

SAND DUNES ARE RARE. MOST DESERTS ARE COVERED IN ROCKS, GRAVEL, OR CRUSTS OF SALT INSTEAD.

A **desert** is **anywhere that receives less than 10 inches (25 cm) of rain in a year.** That means that the **whole of Nevada,** the **driest state,** is **technically a desert.**

CAN HUMAN ACTIVITY CAUSE DESERTS?

In the 13th century, people in part of Poland cut all the trees down. The topsoil blew away, leaving behind 12 square miles (32 km^2) of sand — the Bledow desert. This same kind of process is making many of the world's natural deserts larger today.

 **WRONG!** Trees produce most of the world's oxygen.

ABOUT 1/2 OF THE OXYGEN IN THE ATMOSPHERE IS MADE BY PHYTOPLANKTON, MICROSCOPIC ORGANISMS THAT FLOAT IN SEAWATER.

A lot of the **phytoplankton** is made up of **one type of bacteria called** *Prochlorococcus.* **A gallon (3.8 liters) of seawater contains 400 million of them.**

All of the world's **phytoplankton** is **in the ocean's top 650–980 feet (200–300 m). Below that there is not enough** sunlight for photosynthesis.

Some **phytoplankton photosynthesize like plants** but also **gobble up tiny bits of food from the water** like an animal.

WHERE DOES OXYGEN COME FROM?

Trees and phytoplankton make oxygen by photosynthesis. They take carbon dioxide and water and combine them using the energy from sunlight to make glucose sugar and some oxygen. The glucose is the plant's fuel. The oxygen is a waste product that is released into the air.

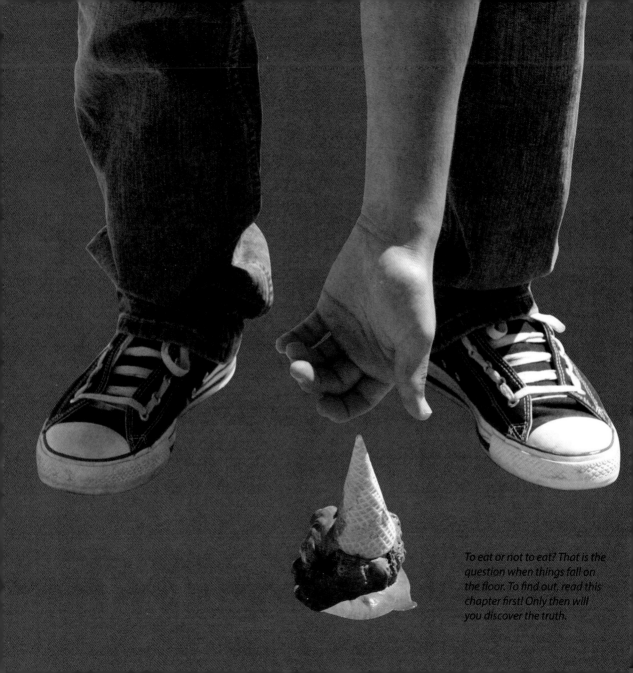

To eat or not to eat? That is the question when things fall on the floor. To find out, read this chapter first! Only then will you discover the truth.

JUST PLAIN WRONG!

In 1929, the Fleer Corporation trained "blowing teachers" to show people how to make bubbles with their new Dubble Bubble gum.

 **WRONG!** If you swallow chewing gum, it takes seven years to digest.

YOUR DIGESTIVE SYSTEM IS SO EFFICIENT THAT GUM TAKES ONLY HOURS, OR DAYS AT MOST, TO PASS THROUGH YOUR BODY.

DID YOU KNOW?

- The Wise Men gave **baby Jesus** chewing gum! **Frankincense** is an African resin and people once chewed it.

- **Maine Pure Spruce Gum**, launched in 1848, was the **first commercial** chewing gum.

- In **Singapore,** gum is only available for **medicinal uses.** It is sugar free and you need to register with a **drug store** to buy it.

TRY THIS! Put some gum in a glass of vinegar and wait for it to dissolve.

 **WRONG!** Different parts of the tongue pick up different tastes.

THE IDEA THAT THE TONGUE HAS A TASTE MAP COMES FROM A TRANSLATION ERROR MADE BY GERMAN SCIENTISTS IN 1901.

People think **the tip picks up sweet tastes,** the **back** detects **bitter flavors,** while **salty and sour** foods are tasted at **the sides. Not so!**

The whole of the tongue can **taste flavors** using little nodules called **taste buds.** There are about **8,000 of them** on the tongue, but they are also found on the **gums** and in the **throat.**

Seeing and smelling **food** **changes** the way you taste it. **Eat blindfolded,** and it is tougher to figure out what **the flavors are.**

Taste buds can't pick up **hot chili.** Instead the **chili triggers a reaction** in the **pain receptors** that makes **your mouth** feel like **it's burning.**

HOW MANY TASTES CAN YOUR TONGUE PICK UP?

There are actually five tastes: sweet, sour, salty, bitter, and umami! Umami means "delicious" in Japanese, and it was only discovered by scientists in the 1980s. Foods that taste of umami include salami, mushrooms, cheese, and tomatoes.

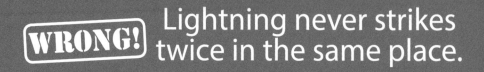

WRONG! Lightning never strikes twice in the same place.

IT IS NOT UNUSUAL FOR THE TOP OF WILLIS TOWER IN CHICAGO TO BE STRUCK TEN TIMES DURING A BIG STORM.

WHAT IS LIGHTNING?

Lightning is a bolt of electricity that flashes through the air during a storm. Storms occur when hot air collides with cold air. The two blocks of air rub against each other, building up static electricity (like a balloon rubbing on a sweater). Eventually, the static charge hurtles toward the ground as an electric current. The electricity in one bolt of lightning is enough to turn on 240,000 light bulbs.

Earth is hit by 3.8 million lightning bolts every day. That's about 1.4 billion strikes a year.

Lightning normally hits **the tallest object** around, such as a tree or a skyscraper. That's the quickest way for it to reach the ground.

Tall buildings have **lightning conductors.** These are thick wires that carry **an electric current** safely from the top of the building to the ground.

Benjamin Franklin is said to have used a kite to catch lightning so it could charge up an **early form of electric battery.** Several people have died copying this experiment.

Some bacteria are **germs** — **tiny living things** that cause **disease.**
Thousands of them could fit on the **period at the end of this sentence.**

The **sink, drain, and faucets** in your kitchen have **more
bacteria** in them than a **toilet** after **flushing!** However, the **few
bugs** that **are in a toilet** are much more likely to make you **sick.**

 **WRONG!**

If you rescue your food from the floor within five seconds, it's still clean.

GERMS DON'T MOVE, SO THEY WON'T CRAWL ONTO YOUR FOOD. BUT HOW CLEAN IS THE FLOOR?

The **human body** is **full of bacteria** already. Roughly **100 trillion of them live in the intestines.** Most are **harmless** and many of them help us **stay healthy.**

A tub of yogurt is full of bacteria even before you spill it on the floor. Yogurt is made by letting harmless bacteria turn milk into a thick, tasty goo.

Colds and upset stomachs are caused by **even tinier bugs, called viruses.** Viruses pass from one person to another as they **touch things** that **others** have **touched,** like door handles.

 **The moon landing was a hoax.**

NOT TRUE! IN 2012, PROBES ORBITING THE MOON TOOK PHOTOS OF THE SPACECRAFT LEFT ON ITS SURFACE.

HOW LONG DOES IT TAKE TO GET TO THE MOON?

The *Apollo* spacecraft took three and a half days to fly through space to the moon. The first crew stayed there for about 22 hours. The last crew, *Apollo 17*, stayed on the surface for three days before flying home.

DID YOU KNOW?

- **The flag** appears to **flap,** as if in a breeze, but is made of **tin foil** and **purposely crumpled** to look that way.

- There is **no wind or rain on the moon,** so the **astronauts' footprints** will stay there **for millions of years.**

- The *Apollo* **astronauts** collected 842 pounds (382 kg) of moon rocks. They are **covered in tiny craters** that are not seen on rocks found on Earth.

WRONG!

Planes discharge
waste from onboard
toilets, leaving
a trail of blue ice.

Aircraft toilets
are often filled with a colored
cleaning fluid, **not clear
water.** It looks **blue,** but
is still filled with yucky
human waste.

In 1971, a **large chunk of ice** from an **airplane**
smashed the roof of a church in London. The building was
too old to fix and had to be **torn down.**

AIRCRAFT ARE NOT ALLOWED TO DUMP SEWAGE MID-FLIGHT. HOWEVER, WASTE TANKS HAVE BEEN KNOWN TO SPRING A LEAK! THE LIQUID FREEZES IN THE VERY COLD AIR.

More than **3.1 billion passengers** travel on airliners every year, aboard **32 million flights.** Even so, there are only about **25 reports of airplane ice** every year.

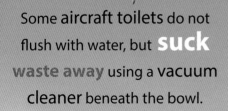

Most of the time, waste is pumped out of the tank after the airplane lands.

Some **aircraft toilets** do not flush with water, but **suck waste away** using a **vacuum cleaner** beneath the bowl.

41

WRONG! Swimming after eating gives you cramps!

IF YOU'VE EATEN A BIG LUNCH, YOU WON'T FEEL LIKE SWIMMING, BUT IF YOU DID GO FOR A DIP, YOU'D BE FINE.

When you swim (or do other exercise), the body sends **more blood to the muscles.** The **cramping myth** comes from the idea that **a full stomach** will keep too much of the **blood supply,** and the muscles will **stop working.**

Swimming on a full stomach is seldom fun. **Blood** rushes away **to the muscles** and any **half-digested food** left sloshing around makes you **feel nauseous.**

People often get **a side stitch** when **exercising after eating.** This could be because **the gut is full of food** and bounces around more than usual.

A **cramp** is when a muscle gets stiff and **won't relax.** Muscle cramps are most common when people **are sleeping.**

If you get a cramp **while playing sports,** it might be because a **muscle** does not have the right mix of chemicals to **contract and relax.**

Will eating carrots improve my eyesight? Lots of people say so, but that doesn't mean it's true. Read on to learn to tell fact from fiction.

EVERYBODY THINKS SO!

Around **two-thirds of men** lose some of their **head hair** as they grow older. Weirdly, this process is **caused by the same hormone** (body chemical) that **makes them grow more hair** on the **face and body.**

Hair grows about **5 inches (13 cm) a year.** It **grows fastest in summer.**

A black hair is about **ten times** thicker than a **blonde** one.

 **WRONG!** Shaving makes hair grow back thicker and quicker.

WHETHER A MOUSTACHE, A BEARD, OR THE WHOLE HEAD, SHAVING WON'T INCREASE THE NUMBER OF HAIRS YOU HAVE.

In the 19th century, **the brushes** used for **applying shaving soap** were made from **supersoft badger fur.**

WHY DO WE THINK SHAVING THICKENS HAIR?

By the time a teenage boy needs to start shaving, his face is becoming naturally hairier anyway. So as he gets older, his facial hair grows thicker and bushier. That would happen whether he shaved or not!

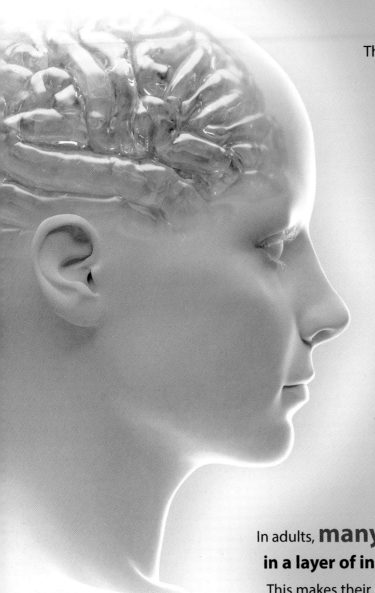

There are **86 billion cells** in an **adult human brain.**

When you are **born,** most of your **brain cells are not connected up** properly. That is why babies can't **walk or talk** as soon as they **are born.**

A toddler grows **one million new brain cells** every four minutes! However, it takes **15 years** for a human brain to start working fully.

In adults, **many nerve fibers** are **coated in a layer of insulation** (called a myelin sheath). This makes their **electric signals move faster.**

 **WRONG!** If you kill a brain cell, it can never be replaced.

THINK AGAIN!
BRAIN EXPERTS
NOW KNOW THAT NEW
BRAIN CELLS GROW
THROUGHOUT YOUR
LIFETIME.

Every **memory** is stored as a **network** of **brain cells.** If you don't **recall a memory,** the **network** will **shrink and disappear.** And you forget the **memory!**

Nerve fibers work like tiny wires that send signals as pulses of electricity. They carry information all over the body.

49

 **WRONG!** You should drink eight glasses of water per day.

SURE, DRINK WATER WHEN YOU FEEL THIRSTY, BUT THERE IS NO NEED TO DRINK THE SAME FIXED AMOUNT EACH DAY.

Long-distance runners are **more likely to get sick** from drinking **too much water** than **not enough!**

DO ATHLETES NEED FLUIDS?

In a test, scientists gave athletes different quantities of water by pumping it straight into their blood. The athletes did not know how much water they had been given, and they all performed equally well. Drinking makes athletes feel less tired, but it doesn't make them any stronger.

There is **no fresh water supply in space.** The **International Space Station** crew cleans all the **waste water** — including **urine** — and **drinks that!**

When **playing most sports,** there is **no need to stop** to take a drink. In a **marathon,** however, **racers** should **drink a cup** every half hour of the race.

WRONG! Goldfish can only remember things for three seconds.

FOR FISH, GOLDFISH HAVE VERY GOOD MEMORIES. THEY CAN REMEMBER THINGS FOR AS LONG AS A YEAR.

Goldfish come to the surface **begging for food** when their owners appear, which shows they can **recognize people.**

Scientists have **trained** goldfish to **find food in mazes,** and to come in response to sound.

Goldfish will learn to push a lever to get **food.** If the **lever only works for one hour a day,** the goldfish **will only push it at that time.**

Goldfish aren't just **gold!**
They can be **yellow,**
white, black, and
multicolored.

In China, yellow goldfish
could only be owned by the
emperor — yellow was
the **imperial color**.

Goldfish
can live for
10–20
years in
captivity.

Liquid-crystal displays — the **screens** on our **computers, TVs, and phones** — **use chemicals** that **change color** when **electrified. Liquid crystals** were first made about **125 years ago** using a **chemical in carrots.**

DID YOU KNOW?

- **Carrots** are **good for your eyes.** They have a lot of **vitamin A,** which is used to make the **light-sensitive chemicals in your retina.**

- The **orange chemical** in a carrot is called **carotene.** It is also one of the **chemicals** that makes **leaves look brown in fall.**

- Eating too many carrots can make your **skin go a little yellow.**

 Carrots improve
your vision.

THEY ARE GOOD FOR
YOU, BUT THEY DO NOT
MAKE YOU SEE BETTER.
THE IDEA COMES FROM
A TRICK PLAYED BY THE
ROYAL AIR FORCE IN
WORLD WAR II.

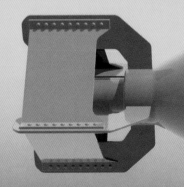

British war planes detected
enemy bombers in the dark
using a new invention: radar.
To keep this secret, they said
pilots ate a lot of carrots to
improve their night vision.

 **WRONG!** Dinosaurs are giant lizards.

PICTURES SHOW DINOSAURS COVERED IN LIZARD-LIKE SCALES, BUT RECENT FOSSIL FINDS REVEAL THAT MANY HAD FEATHERS INSTEAD!

New ways of **studying dinosaur skin** have shown that many species would have had **bright colorful patterns,** and were **not** all **simply** gray **and brown,** as most pictures show.

Dinosaurs like *Tyrannosaurus rex* and *Triceratops* probably had **feathers** for at least part of their lives.

Dinosaur **feathers** were **not** used for **flying.** Instead they were **fluffy** and mostly served to keep an animal **warm.**

A feather is made from the **same material** as a **reptile scale.**

HAVE DINOSAURS DISAPPEARED?

It is said that dinosaurs became extinct 65 million years ago, when a giant meteorite crashed into Earth. However, small feathered dinosaurs survived. Today, we call them birds!

 **Pets don't sweat.**

ANIMALS DO SWEAT, BUT NOT AS MUCH AS A PERSON. HOWEVER, THEY HAVE OTHER WAYS OF STAYING COOL.

DID YOU KNOW?

- **Sweat** is **salty water** that comes out of **tiny holes in our skin** when we get **hot.** It **evaporates,** taking some of the **heat** with it — so we feel **cooler.**

- **Cats** have most of their **sweat glands** on their **paws,** while **hamsters lick their fur** to keep **cool.**

- **Hippos** were thought to **sweat blood!** Actually, they **secrete orange and red liquids,** which act like a **sunscreen** in the **hot African summer.**

A human has **3 million sweat glands.**

Some people get **red in the face** when they are **hot. Their blood** has been **directed to their skin** so it can **give out unwanted heat.**

Dogs pant to **stay cool.** They **stick out their tongues** and **breathe quickly.** The **slobber evaporates** like sweat, **chilling out the dog.**

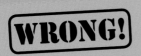 **WRONG!** Public pools use chemicals that change color if you pee.

THIS IS JUST A STORY THAT PARENTS TELL THEIR KIDS SO THEY DON'T GO TO THE BATHROOM WHILE SWIMMING.

Every **swimmer** leaves a **tiny amount of poop, washed off their behinds** by **accident,** when they **go for a swim.** That's why the **pool water** has to be **cleaned.**

WHY DO SWIMMING POOLS SMELL THE SAME?

A swimming pool doesn't smell of the chlorine-containing chemicals used to keep it clean, but of the harmless chemicals that are created once the chlorine has done its job. So, a pool that has a strong "chlorine" smell is actually one that has had the most urine in it!

It would be possible to have a **pee-detecting chemical** in the **water.** However, the **human skin** gives out **similar chemicals** to **those in urine** and these would **change the color** as well.

It is **possible** to get **sick if you swallow** pool water, but don't stop swimming. It could **save your life** one day!

61

Vegans and fruitarians must take **vitamin B$_{12}$ supplements.** The vitamin is only found in **animal products.** A lack can cause **extreme tiredness.**

A **diet** containing too much fatty **meat** will make your **heart unhealthy.**

A **vegan diet** contains **no animal foods from any animal** — no **meat,** milk, cheese, or eggs.

 A vegetarian diet is unhealthy.

A MEAT-FREE DIET CAN BE HEALTHY. JUST EAT PLENTY OF FRUITS, VEGETABLES, AND DAIRY FOODS INSTEAD.

People who eat little or **no meat** and **do not** drink **alcohol** or **smoke** normally **live much longer** than people who do.

Fruitarians only eat the **fruits, seeds, and nuts harvested from living plants.** They **don't want to have to kill** anything for their **food.**

A typical diet in Japan contains a little meat, and plenty of fish and plant foods. The Japanese tend to live longer than most other nations.

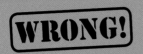 **WRONG!** A penny dropped from a tall building can kill a person.

NO MATTER HOW TALL THE BUILDING, THE PENNY WOULD ONLY FALL AT 11 MPH (18 KPH) — TOO SLOW TO KILL.

If it had a soft place to land, like some thick grass, a mouse could survive falling from an airliner!

A flying squirrel uses a large flap of skin between its front and back legs to increase its drag, so it can glide down to the ground.

In medieval times, armies catapulted rotting horse carcasses over castle walls. They landed with such force that they exploded and spread gunk everywhere.

HOW FAST DO THINGS FALL?

Everything is pulled down to the ground by gravity, while the air around an object creates drag and pushes back the other way. Eventually, the two forces balance out, and an object reaches a steady downward speed. A penny is very light and big for its weight, so it travels more slowly than a large, heavy rock.

Cats have been known to **fall from seven stories** and **survive** — even when they **do not land on their feet!**

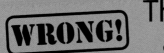 **The moon has a dark side.**

FROM EARTH WE ONLY SEE ONE SIDE OF THE MOON. THE FAR SIDE POINTS AWAY FROM US, BUT IS NOT ALWAYS DARK.

The **near side of the moon** has several **dark patches** known as **"lunar seas."** The **far side of the moon** does not have as many of these, but has more **craters.**

WHY DOES THE MOON CHANGE SHAPE?

Once a month the moon grows from a thin curved shape (crescent moon) to a round disk (full moon) and back again. It appears to change shape because we only see the part lit by the sun. And when no sunlight shines on the moon's face, it looks like there is no moon (new moon).

The first pictures of the **far side of the moon** were taken by _**Luna 3,**_ a **Russian** space probe.

The **moon's largest crater** is on the **far side.** It is called the **Aitken basin** and is big enough to cover most of Europe!

The **moon** goes around Earth once every **29 days,** and **spins** just once in that time. As it **moves** around our planet, the **same side always faces us.**

Can a chameleon blend in with its surroundings? See page 90 to find out. Some explanations are too good to be true. Look closer, and you may find that what you think you know is wrong!

IT'S

COMPLICATED!

 **WRONG!** In Australia, water goes down the drain in an opposite direction than in the U.S.

THIS IS TRUE FOR HUGE CURRENTS IN THE AIR AND THE OCEANS, BUT NOT SO FOR YOUR BATHTUB.

An ocean current generally **flows** in a **huge circle** called a **gyre.** In the **northern hemisphere, gyres** flow **counterclockwise.** In the **south, they flow clockwise.**

Aircraft flying **long distances** are affected by the **Coriolis effect** and have to **adjust their routes** to get to their **destination.**

The **Coriolis effect** has only a **tiny effect** on small things. **A pitched baseball** moves **sideways by the width** of a **fingernail.**

WHAT IS HAPPENING?

Movements in large bodies of air and water are influenced by Earth's rotation from west to east. This means that a wind blowing north in the northern hemisphere will also travel in a counterclockwise direction, while winds blowing south in the southern hemisphere travel in a clockwise direction. This pattern is called the Coriolis effect.

 **WRONG!** Microwaving food in plastic containers causes cancer.

THE PLASTICS USED FOR MAKING "MICROWAVE-SAFE" CONTAINERS HAVE BEEN TESTED TO SHOW THAT THIS DOES NOT HAPPEN.

Regular plastic food packaging **melts** in a microwave.

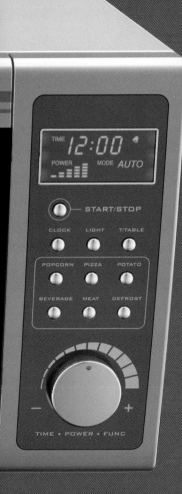

A microwave oven sends a **powerful blast** of radio waves **into the food.** This causes **water and fats to vibrate,** making the food **warm**.

Metal does not heat up in a **microwave,** but **acts a bit like a** lightning conductor. The **microwaves flash** between **metal objects,** creating dangerous sparks.

The microwave oven was invented by accident in the 1940s, when a radar researcher called Percy Spencer found that the radio waves melted a chocolate bar in his pocket.

TIME 12:00

POWER   MODE AUTO

START/STOP

CLOCK   LIGHT   T/TABLE

POPCORN   PIZZA   POTATO

BEVERAGE   MEAT   DEFROST

−   +

TIME • POWER • FUNC

WRONG! The blood in your veins is blue; that in your arteries, red.

BLOOD IS ALWAYS RED, ALTHOUGH BLOOD IN THE ARTERIES IS A LITTLE BRIGHTER THAN BLOOD IN THE VEINS.

Some crabs and lobsters have blood that really does look blue.

Arteries carry blood away from the heart. Nearly all **arteries** are **full** of **bright-red blood** that is **rich** in **oxygen.**

Veins are **tubes** made from **floppy tissue.** They look blue under **pale skin.**

74

Arteries are **tubes** with **muscular walls.** The **muscles contract** to **push the blood along.** You can feel these **contractions** as a **pulse.**

Veins are **nearer** the **surface** of the **skin.** They **carry blood** back to the **heart.** Most of the blood is **deoxygenated,** meaning it has **run out of oxygen.**

The red color in blood comes from an **iron-rich chemical** called **hemoglobin.**

 **According to the laws of physics, bumblebees should be incapable of flight.**

NOTHING CAN BREAK
THE LAWS OF PHYSICS,
AND BUMBLEBEES CAN FLY.
YOU CAN SEE THEM
DO IT EVERY SUMMER!

DID YOU KNOW?

- This **myth** comes from the 1930s, when **scientists compared the wing size and body weight of a bee** with the **laws governing how fixed-wing aircraft flew.**

- A **bumblebee flies more like a helicopter** than an **airplane.**

- **Bumblebees weigh just two-hundredths of an ounce (0.5 g),** but they are **covered in bristles** that make them look **much heavier.**

Bumblebees **steal nectar from some flowers.** They **cut open the base of the flower** to **release its entire supply of sweet liquid** all at once.

Bumblebees live in **underground nests** with up to **400 bees** living in the tunnels.

A **bumblebee's bristles** keep it **warm,** which is why it **can still fly** when it is **too cold** for other bugs, such as butterflies.

This type of **bee** does not make **honey.** Instead, it **feeds its** young with **pollen** and **pure nectar.**

WRONG! There is no gravity in space!

NOT QUITE! IT IS GRAVITY THAT KEEPS EARTH IN ORBIT AROUND THE SUN.

Every object has a **pull of gravity. Earth** is **much bigger** than you are, so **its pull** is much greater.

Astronauts float weightlessly **in space** because they are moving at the **same speed** as everything around them.

Rollercoasters can make you feel weightless as they drive **up** and **over steep** hills. When you **reach the top, you float** in your seat for an instant.

HOW DOES A SPACECRAFT STAY IN ORBIT?

A spacecraft is launched with a powerful rocket that blasts it away from Earth against the pull of gravity. The spacecraft starts to orbit the planet — and is able to stay on course — once its forward motion becomes balanced with Earth's gravity pulling it back down again.

 **Mount Everest is the tallest mountain in the world.**

EVEREST IS THE HIGHEST PEAK ABOVE SEA LEVEL BUT OTHER MOUNTAINS ARE TALLER IN OTHER WAYS.

DID YOU KNOW?

- **Chimborazo,** in Ecuador, is **20,564 feet (6,268 m) tall, while Everest** is 29,035 feet (8,850m). But **Chimborazo** is **located near the Equator,** where **Earth bulges outward.** It means the **peak of Chimborazo is about 7,113 feet (2,168 m) farther from the center of the planet than Everest's.**

- The **top of Mauna Kea,** the volcano on the island of Hawaii, is **13,796 feet (4,205 m) above sea level.** However, when measured from its **base way down on the seafloor, Mauna Kea is 33,465 feet (10,200 m) tall!**

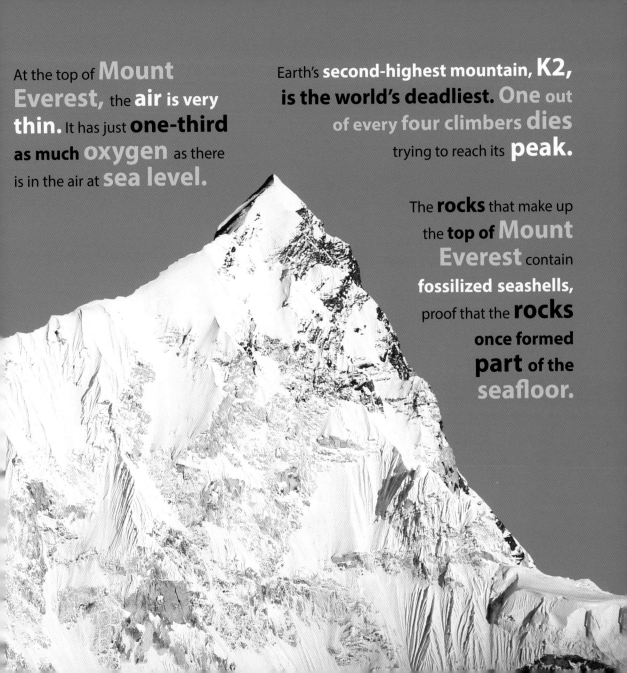

At the top of **Mount Everest,** the **air is very thin.** It has just **one-third as much oxygen** as there is in the air at **sea level.**

Earth's **second-highest mountain, K2, is the world's deadliest. One** out of every four climbers **dies** trying to reach its **peak.**

The **rocks** that make up the **top of Mount Everest** contain **fossilized seashells,** proof that the **rocks** **once formed** **part** of the **seafloor.**

A person having a heart attack feels pain down the left arm.

NOT USUALLY — A PERSON CAN HAVE A HEART ATTACK WITHOUT FEELING ANY PAIN AT ALL.

For a healthy heart, don't be overweight, don't eat too many fatty foods, and do regular exercise that gets the heart pumping fast.

A **heart attack** is when **blood stops** reaching the **heart.** The **heart** does not **stop beating** right away, but **its muscles** stop working properly.

Heart attacks are **not** always **painful.** They can make a person **feel nauseous, numb,** and **light-headed** as well.

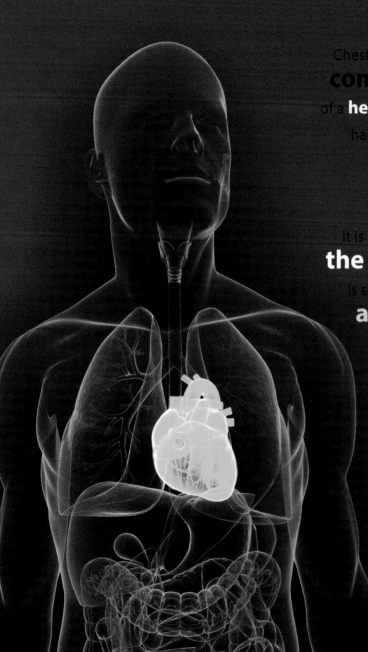

Chest pain and breathlessness are **common symptoms** of a **heart attack,** but not everyone has **those symptoms.**

It is **important to get to the hospital.** If a patient is seen quickly, a **heart attack** may **not cause permanent damage.**

The **heart** is made from **special muscle** that **never** gets **tired out.** It **beats two billion times** in an average lifetime.

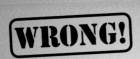

AN EARTHWORM MIGHT SURVIVE BEING CUT IN HALF, BUT IT DOES NOT BECOME TWO WORMS.

If an **earthworm** is **cut between the tail** and the **thick midbody section,** a new tail grows over the severed end. The **old tail end dies.**

Flatworms, which are not related to earthworms, can be cut into many pieces that each grow into a new worm.

An **earthworm's head** is rounder than its tail. If the **worm is cut** between the **head** and its midbody section, **both halves die.**

84

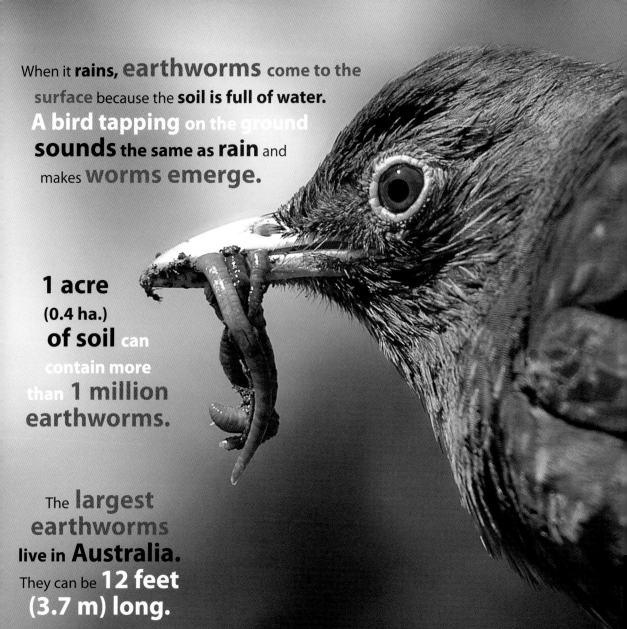

When it **rains, earthworms** come to the surface because the **soil is full of water.** **A bird tapping** on the ground **sounds** the same as **rain** and makes **worms emerge.**

1 acre **(0.4 ha.)** **of soil** can contain more than **1 million earthworms.**

The **largest earthworms** live in **Australia.** They can be **12 feet** **(3.7 m) long.**

 Sharks must swim in order to breathe.

WHILE A FEW SPECIES BREATHE
BEST WHILE SWIMMING,
NEARLY ALL SHARKS
CAN STOP FOR A REST.

The **wobbegong** is a funny sounding Australian shark that **barely swims at all.** It is **disguised** as **seaweed** and **lies still, waiting to ambush** passing fish.

No one is sure if **sharks** go **to sleep.** It is possible that the **brain sleeps** while the **spinal cord** controls the **muscles** so a **shark can swim** and **snooze** at the same time.

Whale sharks use their gills for **feeding** as well as **breathing.** They have **no teeth,** but filter out **plankton** from the water with their **feathery gills.**

HOW DO SHARKS BREATHE?

Most sharks use their throat muscles to pump water through the gills so they can absorb the oxygen mixed in with it. A few types, such as the great white shark, create a flow of water by swimming forward. If the shark stops for too long, it will run out of oxygen and drown.

Breathing while **swimming** is called **ram breathing. Reef sharks** are **ram breathers.** So that they can **rest without swimming,** they look for caves, where the water is **especially high in oxygen.** This **keeps their gills** working.

 **WRONG!** **Earthbound meteors are hot when they hit the ground.**

METEORS GET HOT
AS THEY STREAK
THROUGH EARTH'S
ATMOSPHERE, BUT WHAT'S
LEFT OF THEM AFTER
HITTING THE GROUND IS
ONLY WARM TO THE TOUCH.

Most meteorites are found in Antarctica. It is easier to see the dark rocks against the white ice.

A **meteor** is the **streak** of **light** made by a **burning meteoroid** in the sky. The **rock that hits the ground** is called a **meteorite.**

DID YOU KNOW?

- Before it hits Earth's atmosphere, a **space rock is very cold** — about **−456 °F (−271 °C)**.

- **Friction with the air** makes the **outside of a speeding space rock (meteoroid) get super hot.** The **rock burns away,** creating a **streak of fire.**

- **The friction heating stops as the rock nears the ground,** so it is **not hot when it lands.**

WHAT ARE SHOOTING STARS?

Shooting stars are not really stars. They are tiny meteors — not much more than specks of grit — that burn away completely in the atmosphere. No one knows for sure, but up to 300 tons of dust could come into the atmosphere from space every day!

Some **meteorites** are ancient rocks left over from the **formation** of the **solar system.**

 **Chameleons change color for camouflage.**

THESE COOL LIZARDS CAN CHANGE COLOR, BUT ONLY DO SO WHEN FEELING HOT, COLD, ROMANTIC, OR FRIGHTENED.

Beneath a chameleon's skin are billions of tiny crystals that can be tuned to reflect the **different colors** that **make up light.**

Usually, the **crystals** beneath a chameleon's skin **reflect blue.** The skin is mostly yellow, so the two combine to make the **lizard look green.**

A **chameleon** can retune the **crystals** beneath **its skin** to **change** the mix of colors on **show.**

The chameleon is one of the few animals that can **move** its **eyes independently** of each other. It can look at two things at once.

It takes about a minute for a **chameleon** to **change its body color** completely.

Many other **lizards** can **make** their **skin** lighter and darker.

Stories are fun, but that's all they are. Science presented in movies is very exciting but not always right. Even Newton's apple is not what it seems.

MEDIA MIX-UPS!

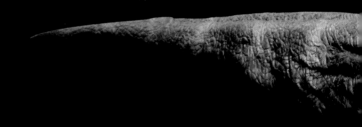

 Humans were around in the age of dinosaurs.

Mammals evolved around the **same time as dinosaurs,** but they were all small animals.

Ancient humans did live beside **woolly rhinos, mammoths, saber-toothed tigers,** and **sloths the size of buses!**

64 MILLION YEARS PASSED BETWEEN THE EXTINCTION OF THE DINOSAURS AND THE FIRST HUMANLIKE CREATURES APPEARING ON EARTH.

Most of the types of **mammals** we see today evolved **30 million years ago.**

The earliest relative of **modern humans** was ***Homo habilis,*** a species that lived in Africa about **two million years** ago.

Modern humans first appeared about **200,000 years ago in Africa.** By **45,000 years ago,** they lived **in all parts of the world, except Antarctica and the Americas.**

The **dinosaurs** were **wiped out** by an **asteroid smashing** into **Earth 66 million years ago.**

WRONG!

Lemmings commit mass suicide.

Lemmings are **relatives of voles.** They live in **cold rocky meadows** that are often **covered in snow.**

Lemmings like to **live in groups,** but when their **meadow gets too crowded,** the **rodents move away** to **find a quieter place to live.**

A NATURE MOVIE FROM 1958 SHOWED LEMMINGS JUMPING OFF A CLIFF. THE CAMERA CREW THREW THEM OVER!

A **female lemming** can **give birth** to **5 babies** per litter. Those **babies have babies of their own** after about seven weeks. It can get **crowded very quickly.**

Lemmings cut grass and dry it as hay so they have something to eat in winter.

HOW DID THE MYTH START?

On rare occasions, wandering lemmings are forced back together — when crowding through a gap between large rocks, for example. This can lead to erratic behavior. The rodents go wild with agitation, dashing blindly in all directions. Some might fall off a cliff in panic, but it's an accident, not suicide.

WRONG! Newton "discovered" gravity when an apple fell on his head.

People knew about gravity **before Isaac Newton —** **the word gravity** was introduced around **200 years before.**

An apple falling from a tree helped Newton see that the **force pulling the apple** to Earth was the **same as the one** that kept the **moon** and **planets** in **orbit.**

Scientists still **measure forces** (like gravity) in units called **newtons.** One **newton** is the **force needed** to **move** 2.2 pounds of mass **3 feet (1 m) in one second.**

HOW DOES GRAVITY WORK?

All objects have a pull of gravity. Big things, like planets, have a much greater gravitational pull than small things, like apples. The size of the force is also affected by distance, and gets weaker the farther away an object is. Scientists use Newton's law of gravitation to figure it all out.

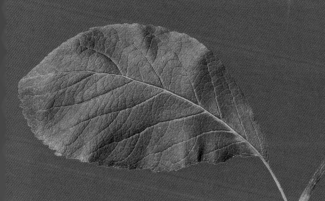

Newton figured out the math that explained how gravity worked and we still **use it today.**

ISAAC NEWTON ONLY TOLD THE APPLE STORY WHEN HE WAS IN HIS 80S — 60 YEARS AFTER HIS WORK ON GRAVITY. HE DID NOT SAY THE APPLE FELL ON HIS HEAD!

 **WRONG!** Elephants have graveyards.

THERE IS NO EVIDENCE OF THIS. HOWEVER, MANY SKELETONS ARE SOMETIMES FOUND IN ONE PLACE.

One of the **earliest "graveyards"** was a **mass of fossil skeletons** of a long-gone European elephant. The animals had been **killed by prehistoric humans.**

Elephants live in families. They **stick together** when **attacked.** The **adults surround** the **children** and **fight off the attackers.**

There are **several reports** of finding many **elephant skeletons in one place.** It is likely they are **families of elephants** that have been **killed** by **hunters.**

ELEPHANT OR CYCLOPS?

The cyclops is a mythical giant with one huge eye. It featured in the stories of ancient Greece. The idea for its appearance may come from an elephant skull, which has a large hole in the middle where the trunk would be. It gives the skull the appearance of having one big eye socket.

 Clones are identical.

IN MOVIES, CLONES ARE MADE IN MACHINES AND ARE IDENTICAL TO THEIR PARENTS. DON'T BELIEVE IT!

THREE CLONING FACTS

- **A clone** is an animal that has been **made in the laboratory,** by copying the genes of another animal — **its "parent."**

- Because it has the **same set of genes as its parent, a clone will look very similar.** But it is **always going to be younger.**

- **Plants** can be **clones, too!** Almost **all the bananas we eat come from clones of a single banana plant,** which was **grown in an English greenhouse in 1834.**

Identical twins, like these lambs, are a natural kind of clone. They have the **same genes,** but there are always **a few tiny differences** between them.

HOW DO GENES WORK?

Genes are instructions on how to make a living body. However, the body they produce is always influenced by the environment in which it grows. For example, the food an animal eats and the diseases it catches will affect how it grows and what it looks like.

Spiders are dangerous, right? Sure, some are, but not this cuddly tarantula. Just because something sounds true, it doesn't mean it actually is.

BUT IT SOUNDS TRUE!

 **WRONG!** Bananas grow
on trees.

A BANANA PLANT GROWS AS TALL AS A TREE, BUT IT IS NOT A TREE. IT HAS NO TRUNK AND IS MADE UP OF GIANT LEAVES.

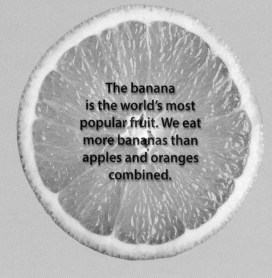

The banana is the world's most popular fruit. We eat more bananas than apples and oranges combined.

DID YOU KNOW?

○ A **banana plant** is an **herb,** more **closely related to parsley than an apple tree.**

○ Bananas grow in **clusters called "hands."** Each **hand** has about **15 "fingers."** Those are the bananas.

○ **Wild bananas** come from **Southeast Asia,** but today most bananas are grown in **South America.**

There is no big difference between a **banana** and a **plantain.** **Bananas** are eaten when they are **soft and sweet,** while **plantains** are **hard** and **must be cooked.**

 **WRONG!** World War I was the biggest cause of death from 1914–1920.

16 MILLION PEOPLE DIED DURING WORLD WAR I. AN OUTBREAK OF INFLUENZA IN 1918 WENT ON TO KILL UP TO 50 MILLION.

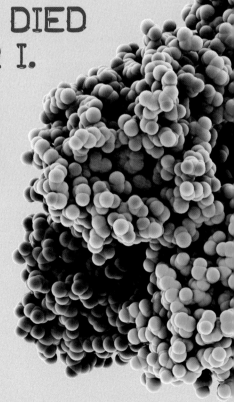

The 1918 **outbreak** was **Spanish flu.** By 1920, it had **spread** all over the world, even to remote Pacific islands.

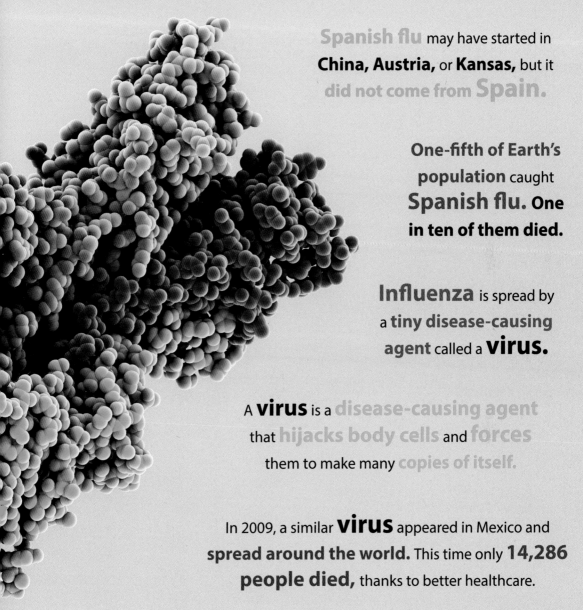

Spanish flu may have started in **China, Austria,** or **Kansas,** but it did not come from **Spain.**

One-fifth of Earth's population caught **Spanish flu. One in ten of them died.**

Influenza is spread by a **tiny disease-causing agent** called a **virus.**

A **virus** is a disease-causing agent that hijacks body cells and forces them to make many copies of itself.

In 2009, a similar **virus** appeared in Mexico and **spread around the world.** This time only **14,286 people died,** thanks to better healthcare.

 **WRONG!** Touching a young bird will cause its mother to reject it.

BIRD PARENTS WORK HARD TO LOOK AFTER THEIR CHICKS AND WILL NOT ABANDON THEM IF A PERSON TOUCHES ONE OF THEM.

Some people think **human contact** will make a chick **smell funny** to its **parents.** In fact, **most birds can't smell very well.**

An adult herring gull has a red spot on its beak. Chicks learn to peck on the spot to tell parents they're hungry.

A mother bird might decide to **abandon** a nest that **has been tampered with.**

A cuckoo lays an egg in another bird's nest. If it goes unnoticed, a mother bird raises the **invader** as one of her own.

A few hours after hatching, ducklings and **chicks** of similar birds learn to follow the **biggest thing they can see** — normally their **mother.**

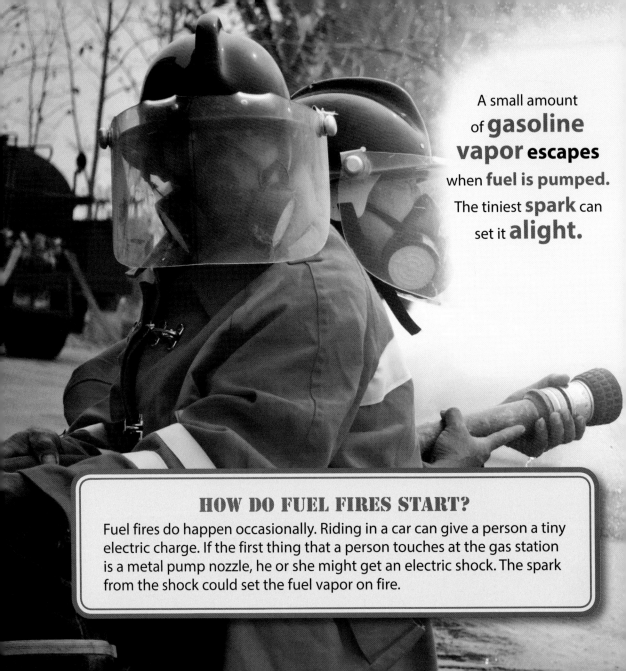

A small amount of **gasoline vapor escapes** when **fuel is pumped.** The tiniest **spark** can set it **alight.**

HOW DO FUEL FIRES START?

Fuel fires do happen occasionally. Riding in a car can give a person a tiny electric charge. If the first thing that a person touches at the gas station is a metal pump nozzle, he or she might get an electric shock. The spark from the shock could set the fuel vapor on fire.

 **Using a cell phone at a gas station could cause a fire.**

NO ONE HAS EVER STARTED A GASOLINE FIRE WITH A CELL PHONE.

In the early days of **cell phones,** people were unsure if **using the gadget** while **pumping fuel** could be **dangerous.**

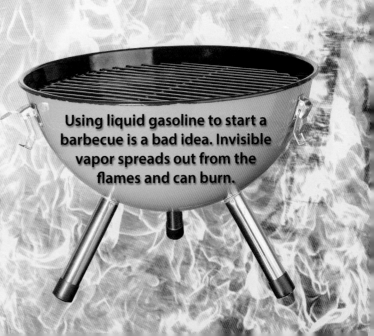

Using liquid gasoline to start a barbecue is a bad idea. Invisible vapor spreads out from the flames and can burn.

Gasoline floats on water. Firefighters cannot use **water** to put out **burning fuels,** but **smother flames** with **foam** or **nonburning gases** instead.

 Sugar makes
kids hyperactive.

IT'S NOT SUGAR THAT MAKES KIDS EXCITABLE; THEY JUST LIKE TO HAVE FUN!

WHAT IS HYPERACTIVITY?

Hyperactive kids have trouble concentrating, sitting still, and being quiet when they need to. Doctors have found that many of these kids have lower amounts of sugar in their blood than normal, not too much!

Kids at birthday parties eat lots of **candy** and get **very** excited about all the **fun. Parents assume** it's because of the sugar, but they're wrong.

Sugar is the **body's main fuel.** The **body stores** it as a **chemical** called **glycogen** and slowly releases it as **glucose** when needed.

Doctors have done **tests** in which they give some children **sugary food** and others the same food **sweetened in other ways. All the kids behave** just **the same** afterward.

People who eat **glucose tablets** before sports are usually **wasting their time.** The **body doesn't need extra glucose** until it has **run out of glycogen.** That takes **two or three hours of hard exercise.**

 **WRONG!** Ostriches stick their heads in the sand.

"STICKING YOUR HEAD IN THE SAND" MEANS IGNORING PROBLEMS, BUT THESE BIG BIRDS ARE TOO SMART FOR THAT.

A **mother ostrich** lays her **huge eggs** in a nest **hole dug into the ground.** She **turns the egg around from time to time** with her beak. From a long way off **it looks as if her head is underground.**

An **ostrich eye** is **twice as big as a human eye,** and can **see much farther,** too.

An **ostrich uses its wings** as **rudders** to **help make sharp turns** as it **races away** from a **predator.**

Ostriches are **6.5 feet** (2 m) **tall.** **They can't fly,** but they sure can **run,** with a **top speed** of **43 miles** an hour (70 km/h).

Ostriches hide from attackers by lying **flat on the ground.** They have **huge claws** for **slashing** if all else fails.

A **male ostrich** has **black feathers;** the **female** has **brown ones.**

The edge of a **black hole** is called the **event horizon.** If you cross that line, you cannot escape the **hole!**

It was the famous scientist **Stephen Hawking** who figured out that **black holes** give out *particles,* now known as **Hawking radiation.**

WRONG! Black holes suck in all the matter around them.

BLACK HOLES HAVE SUPERSTRONG GRAVITY, BUT GIVE OUT MATTER AS WELL AS SUCK IT IN.

If an **astronaut** fell into a **black hole,** he or she would be stretched like elastic when crossing the **event horizon.**

A **black hole** bends space so much that even time is affected and slows down compared with **space farther away.**

WHAT IS HAWKING RADIATION?

Tiny particles constantly come in and out of existence. They come in pairs and disappear again almost immediately. When a pair of particles appears on either side of an event horizon, one goes into the black hole and the other escapes. So, gradually, the black hole gives out particles.

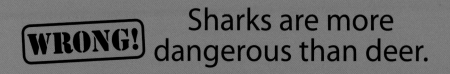

Sharks are more dangerous than deer. **WRONG!**

MOST SHARKS ARE BUILT TO KILL, BUT MANY MORE PEOPLE ARE KILLED BY DEER EACH YEAR.

DID YOU KNOW?

- On average, a **shark kills one American** every year, while **130 people** lose their lives because of deer.

- When sharks attack, it's often because they think the **swimmer is a seal**. People taste wrong, so they **spit them out**.

- **Deer kill people in car crashes.** Big deer, like **moose,** are the **most dangerous because they are so heavy.**

There are **thousands** of **shark attacks** each year around the world, but only about **6 people die** from them.

Deer are America's most **dangerous** animals. The **most dangerous** animal in Japan is the **giant hornet.** The **venom** in just **30 stings** is **enough to kill a person.**

Humans kill about **100 million sharks** every year! Mostly, they are **hunted for their fins,** which are used in **Chinese soups.**

 **WRONG!** Tarantulas are deadly.

A TARANTULA'S VENOMOUS BITE IS NO WORSE THAN A WASP STING.

A New World **tarantula flicks barbed hairs** from its body at **attackers.** They are **painful** if they strike the **eyes** or **lips.**

The **largest tarantula** is the **goliath bird-eater.** It is **12 inches (30 cm) across.** Despite the name, it **eats worms.**

WHAT DOES THE NAME TARANTULA MEAN?

European explorers to America thought these spiders resembled a smaller, unrelated spider local to the city of Taranto, Italy. In the 13th century, a bite from this spider was said to make victims dance wildly, and inspired a fast dance called the tarantella. Tarantulas are named after the dance.

African **tarantulas** are known as **baboon spiders.** These are **more dangerous** than most other species. A **bite** makes you feel **nauseous.**

In Australia, **tarantulas** are called **whistling spiders.** They **hiss** at people.

Female **tarantulas** **live** for **thirty years.** A **male** **lives** for less than **ten.**

 Polar bears have white hair.

IT SEEMS SO, BUT IF YOU COULD GET VERY CLOSE, YOU'D SEE THE HAIRS ARE COLORLESS.

THREE HAIRY FACTS

- A **polar bear's hairs** are **hollow and filled with air.** That makes them even better at **insulating the animal in the cold.**

- Beneath **all of its hair,** a polar bear's skin is **black.**

- Most mammal hairs contain a **mixture of three pigments.** When these pigments fade away, the **hair goes gray** and then **completely white.**

Polar bears have very **large feet** for **walking** on **snow. They use them** as **paddles** when **swimming** through the **ocean.**

A grizzly bear is named after **its "grizzled" hair.** The hair shafts are **brown,** but their tips are a **silvery gray.**

INDEX

Why do gulls have red spots on their beaks?

Did an appple help Newton discover gravity?

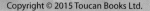

This edition published by Scholastic Inc., 557 Broadway, New York, NY 10012
by arrangement with Toucan Books Ltd.

Author: Tom Jackson
Managing Editor: Ellen Dupont
Designer: Carol Davis
Editor: Anna Southgate
Picture Researcher: Sharon Southren
Consultant: Dr. Kathy Weston
Proofreader: Marion Dent
Indexer: Marie Lorimer

ISBN: 978-0-545-83530-5

10 9 8 7 6 5 4 3 2 1   08 09 10 11 12

Printed in Guangzhou, China.

PICTURE CREDITS